Picture Bracelet Basics

Parts of a Bracelet

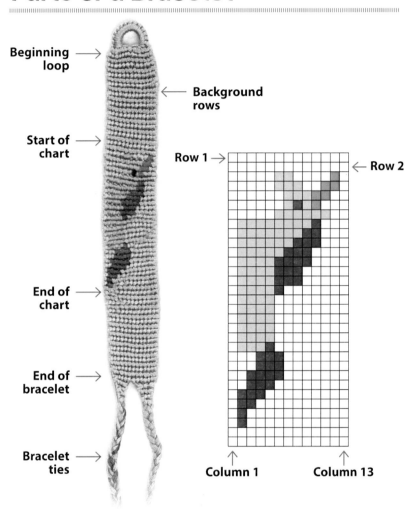

Beginning loop →

← Background rows

Start of chart →

Row 1 →

← Row 2

End of chart →

End of bracelet →

Bracelet ties →

↑ Column 1   ↑ Column 13

Basic Supplies

Materials

Floss in assorted colors (6-ply embroidery floss, pearl [perle] cotton size 5, or craft strands, such as those by DMC®, Anchor®, or Prism®)

Tools

- Tape (masking, duct, packing, or quilter's)
- Safety pin
- Scissors
- Hard knotting surface (any flat, sturdy surface you can apply tape to, such as a clipboard or knotting board)
- Soft knotting surface (a pillow, jeans pantleg, etc.)

Optional Supplies

- Needle with a large eye (size #20 tapestry needle works best), for troubleshooting
- Anti-fraying solution (like June Tailor® Fray Block™), for gluing the ends of the strands
- Clothespin with spring or bodkin, for keeping the knotting strand untangled

Reading Charts

The thing that makes picture bracelets different from other friendship bracelets is the charts used to knot the designs. It might sound tricky at first, but once you've knotted your first motif each new picture after that gets easier.

- Each square represents two knots on the background strands of floss.
- Work the first row from left to right and the second row from right to left. Continue this pattern for the rest of the bracelet (see chart above).
- When the color changes on the chart, switch to using the background strand of floss to make the knots (see page 6).
- It's easy to skip a row, so be careful! Mark a row complete by crossing it out with a pencil or use a sticky note to cover rows you've completed (see Troubleshooting on page 16).
- Charts are shown vertically, so they are in the same position as you're working.
- Rows are side to side and columns are top to bottom on the charts shown.

This book shares dozens of designs beginning on page 20, as well as extra blank charts you can use to make your own custom designs (see the inside back cover).

Determining Bracelet Sizes

The length and width of a bracelet depend on a bunch of different factors. With a tape measure and your picture chart, you can have a bracelet that fits just right in a few simple steps.

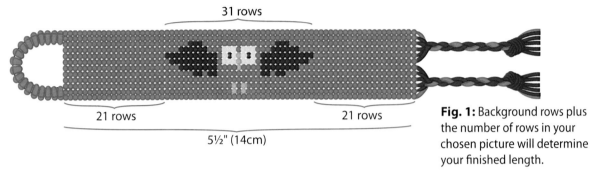

31 rows

21 rows   21 rows

5½" (14cm)

Fig. 1: Background rows plus the number of rows in your chosen picture will determine your finished length.

Length

While a bracelet's length depends somewhat on how tightly you knot, most bracelets are between 5" and 6" (12.7 and 15.2cm) long, not including the loop or braided ties on either end. The overall length is determined by the design you choose, plus the number of background rows before and after your letters. For most, 12–14 rows will equal about 1" (2.5cm) of the bracelet.

To customize the length, wrap a tape measure around your wrist (or a friend's wrist). This is how long you will want the finished bracelet to be (again, not including the loop and braided ties). Use the chart below to decide how many rows you need for your bracelet length.

Bracelet Length	Total Number of Rows
5" (12.7 cm)	60–70 rows
5¼" (13.3cm)	63–74 rows
5½" (14cm)	66–77 rows
5¾" (14.6cm)	69–81 rows
6" (15.2cm)	72–84 rows

Next, count how many rows are in the picture you want to knot. Once you know the number of rows, you can look for your size on the chart above and see how many background rows you need to add to reach your finished length. If you're using a small motif that is going to be repeated, remember to count an extra one or two rows between each motif.

The example bracelet of the Flying Owl (**fig. 1**) is 31 rows long, which means you need to add 34–46 extra background rows to have a 5½" (14cm)–long bracelet. To center the picture on the bracelet, split the number of background rows in half. This tells you how many rows go before the picture and how many go after, which in this case, is 21 before and 21 after.

Width

The width of your bracelet is determined by the size of the picture chart you use. Wider bracelets use tall pictures while narrow bracelets use shorter motifs. (See the picture charts starting on page 20) The width is also affected by the number of border rows you add. All bracelets should have at least one border row on each side of the picture you're knotting. But don't feel limited to just one! You can add two or more border rows if you'd like a wider finished design.

To add borders to your pictures, simply add extra strands to the start of your bracelet. For example, if your design is ten boxes wide on the chart and you want to add one border row to each side, you start with 12 strands. If your design is only five boxes wide on the chart and you want to add two border rows on each side, start with seven strands. All the charts in this book are shown with one border row, so add an extra border row on each side to any chart you want (**fig. 2**).

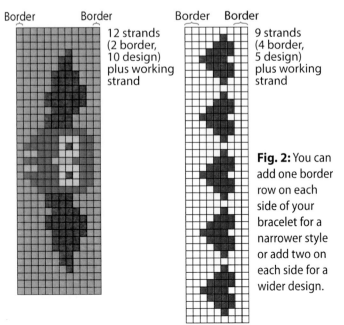

Border   Border

12 strands (2 border, 10 design) plus working strand

Border   Border

9 strands (4 border, 5 design) plus working strand

Fig. 2: You can add one border row on each side of your bracelet for a narrower style or add two on each side for a wider design.

Knotting Bracelet Designs

Like traditional friendship bracelets, picture bracelets use forward and backward knots worked row by row to create the finished pattern. Before starting your first bracelet, review the basic knots to refresh your memory and set yourself up for success.

Determining Floss Needed

The bracelet charts in this book range between three rows and ten rows and include one border row on each edge. So, depending on the design you are knotting, you would need anywhere from 3 to 6 strands of floss (each strand of floss is doubled over to create two rows). If you want extra border rows to make a wider bracelet, add one strand per border (border strands, like background/pictures strands, are folded in half to create a border row on each side of the bracelet).

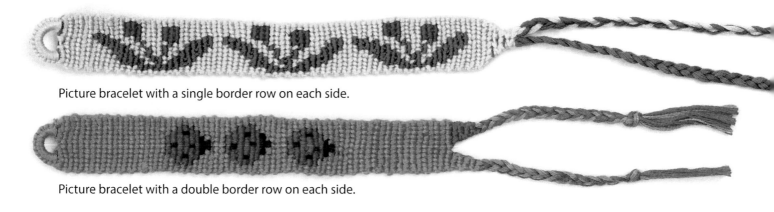

Picture bracelet with a single border row on each side.

Picture bracelet with a double border row on each side.

Knotting on Hard and Soft Surfaces

One of the best things about making friendship bracelets is that you can knot them almost anywhere. You will need tape and a hard surface to make the beginning loop, but once you finish that, take your bracelet with you on the go. Once your loop is complete, you can use a safety pin to anchor your bracelet to a pillow or another soft surface (like the pantleg of your jeans).

If you're working with different color strands that need to be pulled to the back and front of the design at different points in your knotting, securing the top of the bracelet with a glass or novelty head pin enables you to wind the non-working strands around the pins to keep them out of the way (**fig. 1**). If you choose to secure the top of the bracelet with tape to a hard surface, lift up the ends of the tape to secure the non-working strands (**fig. 2**).

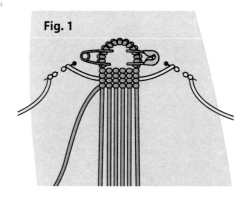

Fig. 1

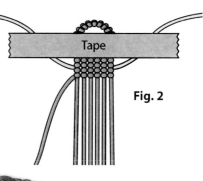

Tape

Fig. 2

Bracelets with an Even Number of Columns

Basically, if your picture bracelet has a single border on each side and has an even number of rows, start by cutting 1 strand for the borders and 1 strand for every *two* background/picture rows (**fig. 1**).

For example, when starting a ten-column bracelet (with one border row on each side), cut:

- 4 strands 48" (121.92cm) long from your background or picture floss color
- 1 strand 48" (121.92cm) long from your border floss color

Your border will generally be cut from the same color (or a similar color) as your background/working strand. The interior bracelet strands may be cut from the same color as your background, but generally, you will start with the first picture color that is introduced into your design. Take a look at the chart to see which colors are introduced first. Depending on the picture chart, cut the interior bracelet rows from a picture floss color rather than a background floss color. See Picture Strands and Changing Colors on page 10 for more on this.

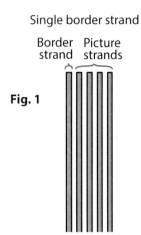

Single border strand

Border Picture
strand strands

Fig. 1

Bracelets with an Odd Number of Columns

The easiest way to work with an odd number of columns is to treat them as if it were even with one extra. For example, if your chart has nine columns, you'll cut enough floss for it to be ten columns wide. Then, while knotting your first row, knot two strands together as if they are one.

Make your beginning loop over all ten rows using the knotting floss. As you begin knotting (as described on page 10), knot over a border strand, 6 single strands, and one group of doubled strands treated as one, and the final border strand, resulting in nine knots across (**fig. 1**). Once you have knotted four to five rows of your bracelet, clip out the extra strand (**fig. 2**).

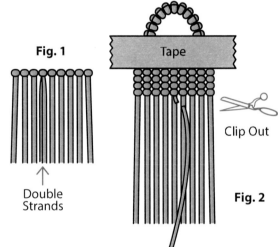

Fig. 1

Tape

Clip Out

Double
Strands

Fig. 2

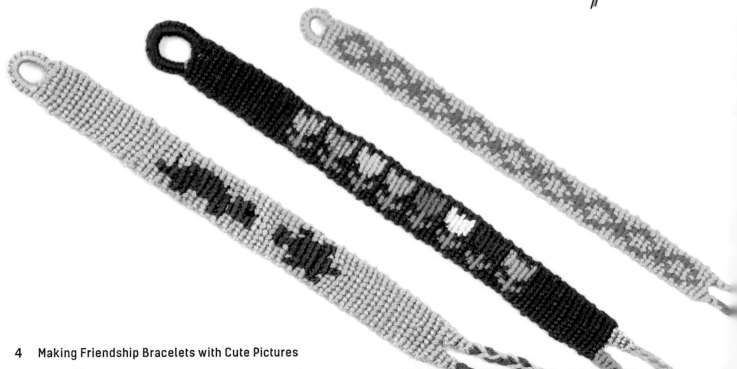

Basic Knots

Here are a few of the basic knots used to make the bracelets in this book. Refer back to this section if you need a refresher on the techniques.

Forward Knot (FK)

All FK will move from *left to right*.

Always *tie two HH for each FK or BK before moving on to the next strand. If you make only one, your bracelet will be very loose, and the sides will curve. The exception to this rule is when making the starting loop. There, you begin with a complete FK/BK, then continue, alternating FHH and BHH.*

1 Bring the leftmost working strand (background floss) over and then under the strand immediately to the right of it. Pull the end of the working strand through the loop that has formed. Tug until the knot is firmly against the previous row of knots. This is called a half-hitch knot (HH) (**fig. 1**) and when done with an FK, it's called a forward half-hitch knot (FHH).

2 Repeat by tying a second FHH using the same working strand. Pull the second FHH up firmly against the first (**fig. 2**).

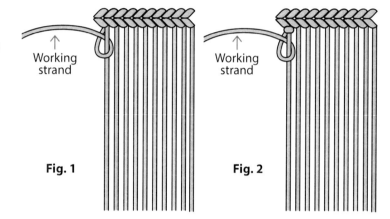

Fig. 1   **Fig. 2**

Backward Knot (BK)

All backward knots (BK) will move from *right to left*.

1 Bring the rightmost working strand (background floss) over and then under the strand immediately to the left of it. Pull the end of the working strand through the loop that has formed for a BK. Tug until the knot is firmly against the previous row of knots for an HH (**fig. 1**). When done with a BK, it's called a backward half-hitch knot (BHH).

2 Repeat by tying a second BHH using the same working strand. Pull the second knot up firmly against the first (**fig. 2**).

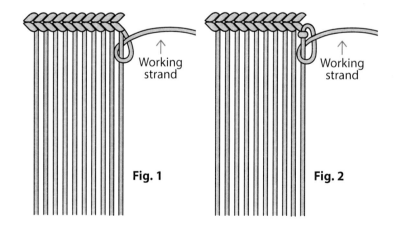

Fig. 1   **Fig. 2**

Overhand Knot (OK)

The overhand knot (OK) is a very simple knot that almost everyone knows how to do. Gather all the strands as one and tie a simple knot, like you would at the end of a hand-sewing thread.

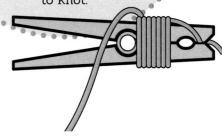

Knotting a Reverse Color over Background Strand

To create the pictures, instead of knotting the background strand over the picture base strand, you will be knotting the picture base strands over the background strand. The process is the same as creating an FK or BK with the background floss, depending on which direction you're working; however, when working an FK (working left to right), how you hold the strand and pull it tight determines how nicely your knots finish.

1 Lay the background strand over the picture base strand. Loop the picture base strand over and through the loop that has formed (**fig. 1**).

2 With the background strand in your left hand and the picture base strand in your right, cross your hands and pull in opposite directions so the picture strand color is visible as you tighten the knot (**fig. 2**). Make a second HH using the same technique to complete your FHH.

3 For creating the picture design with a BK (working right to left), lay the background strand over the adjacent picture strand. Pass the picture strand over then under and through the loop and tighten so the picture floss color is visible as you knot (**fig. 3**). Make a second HH using the same technique to complete your BHH.

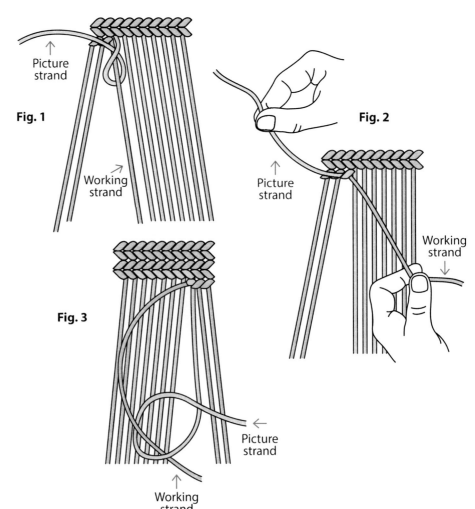

Picture strand

Working strand

Fig. 1

Picture strand

Fig. 2

Working strand

Fig. 3

Picture strand

Working strand

Starting a Bracelet

For the bracelets you'll be making with this book, select one skein for the background strand color and the required number for your picture.

Whether you're using a hard or soft surface to create your bracelet, you will need masking tape or packing tape to create the top loop (pictured at right). Once your loop is complete, you can use a safety pin to anchor your bracelet to a pillow or soft surface (even the leg of your jeans) if you prefer.

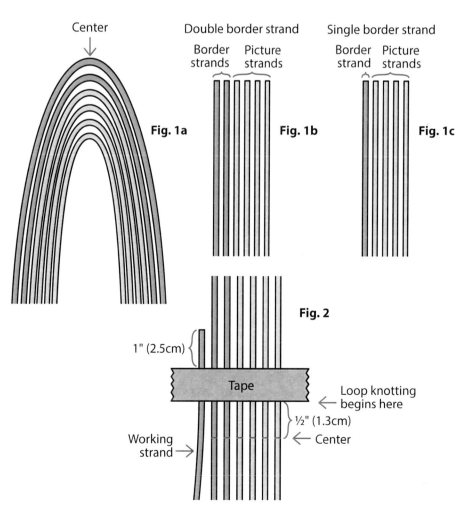

Supplies

- From your picture color, when using the wide-band picture graphs, cut 4 strands at 48" (122cm) long
- From your background color, for a single border at the edges, cut 1 strand 48" (122cm) long (or cut 2 strands 48" [122cm] long, for a double border at the edges)
- Basic supplies (see page 1)

Beginning Loop

The following steps are for a bracelet with an even number of rows. If your bracelet requires an odd number, you can still follow these instructions. The final steps will get you to the odd number you need.

1 Determine the number of strands needed and cut your floss. Place the 48" (122cm) strands together and find the center point by folding them in half (**fig. 1a**). Make sure the 2 border strands are on the left side for a double border (**fig. 1b**) or 1 border strand on the left side for a single border (**fig. 1c**).

The illustrations from step 3 to the end will only show a bracelet with 2 border strands.

2 On a hard work surface, tape the strands down so that the lower edge of your tape is approximately ½" (1.3cm) above the center point determined in step 1. Pull up the left side of the tape and align the starting end of the working strand to the left side of your strands, and at least 1" (2.5cm) above the top edge of the tape. Secure with tape again (**fig. 2**).

Center
↓

Double border strand
Border strands / Picture strands

Single border strand
Border strand / Picture strands

Fig. 1a   Fig. 1b   Fig. 1c

Fig. 2

1" (2.5cm)

Tape

Loop knotting
← begins here

½" (1.3cm)
← Center

Working
strand →

3 With the working strand, knot an FHH over *all* of the strands and secure tightly (**fig. 3a**). Then work a second FHH over *all* of the strands (**fig. 3b**). Work a BHH over all of the strands and secure (**fig. 3c**). Continue alternating FHH and BHH for ¾" (2cm) for a smaller loop or 1" (2.5cm) for a larger loop (**fig. 3d**).

Refer to Basic Knots on page 5 for detailed instructions on how to make each knot and the abbreviations.

Tip
Some people just naturally make knots tighter and some people naturally make knots looser. As long as the knots are secure and consistent, both are correct. Consistent tension is what makes a pretty bracelet.

Loop Lengths
This chart shows the loop length when straightened and laid flat, approximate number of HH needed, and how much length each size loop adds to your bracelet's overall size.

Loop Size	Loop Length (straightened)	Approx. No. Knots	Length Added
Small	¾" (2cm)	20 knots	¼" (0.6cm)
Large	1" (2.5cm)	30 knots	½" (1.3cm)

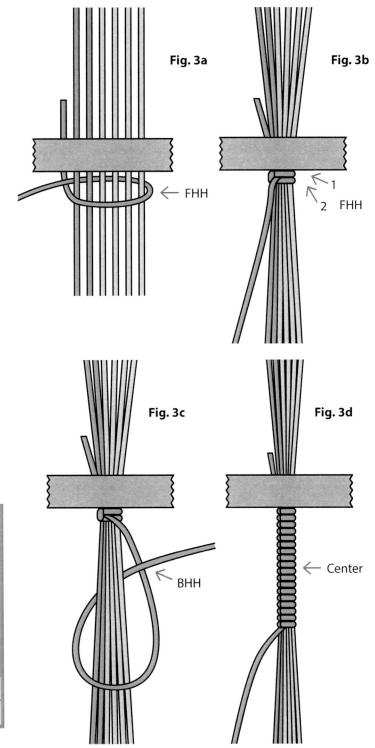

Fig. 3a

Fig. 3b

← FHH

1
2 FHH

Fig. 3c

Fig. 3d

← BHH

← Center

4 Remove the tape and fold so the knotted loop is even and the center point is at the top (**fig. 4**). Check that your strands are approximately the same length at the bottom. If one side is noticeably longer than the other, hold all the strands (*except* the working strand) and carefully slide the knotted loop section until it's centered on your strands.

5 Secure the loop with tape on a board or pin to the chosen surface and begin knotting the bracelet according to the design. For designs with an odd number of rows, begin knotting over the first border strand then knot over 2 or 3 single picture base strands. Knot the next 2 picture base strands together as 1 strand (**fig. 5**). Finishing knotting single strands to finish the row. You will also have a short tail at the bracelet edge from your knotting skein; you will want to catch this tail in a few rows of background knotting before cutting off the excess.

6 Once you've knotted a few rows, clip off one of the doubled picture base strands from step 5, so that you have the required number strands for you graph (**fig. 6**).

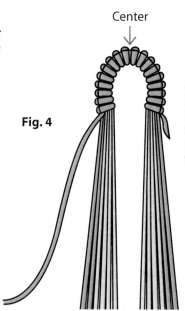

Center

Make a loop with a knotted section of border threads on the outside and picture threads in the center

Fig. 4

Tape and begin knotting the number of background rows needed before your chart begins →

Tip
Although it's easier to use a hard surface to knot a bracelet, you can knot on a soft surface like a pillow as well. Use a safety pin to attach the beginning loop to your soft surface.

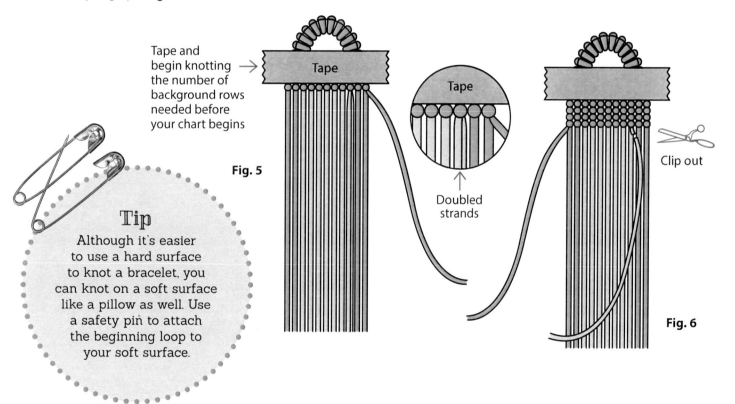

Tape

Fig. 5

Tape

Doubled strands

Clip out

Fig. 6

Picture Strands and Changing Colors

Since you arrange your floss before you make the beginning loop, the way you approach a picture bracelet depends on the design you choose—how many color changes are involved, the way it is charted, and how you prefer to work.

This section will discuss four different approaches and levels of difficulty. You may end up doing a combination of these techniques in a single bracelet, but these four approaches should cover any bracelet design.

Basic Bracelets

Basic geometric picture bracelets with only two color strands can be arranged before you start to knot so that the color that appears in your chart corresponds to the floss color(s) you choose for your picture strands. To help explain this technique, imagine you're working a green pattern on a blue background.

1 Cut your border thread (**fig. 1**). You will only need to cut 2 strands of green floss and 1 border strand of blue floss.

2 Arrange the blue and green strands (**fig. 2a**). When you make your top loop (see page 7) and fold it in half, you will end up with a blue border strand on each side and green picture strands in the center (**fig. 2b**). Simply follow the design's graph. As long as you cut the strands long enough in the beginning, there should be no need to introduce any additional strands or colors.

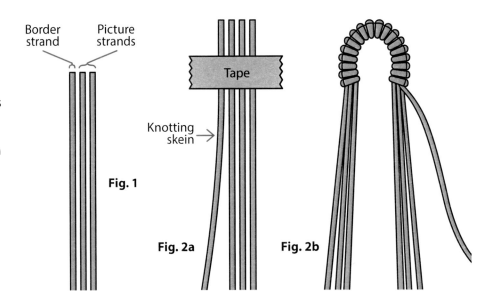

Border strand · Picture strands

Tape

Knotting skein →

Fig. 1

Fig. 2a **Fig. 2b**

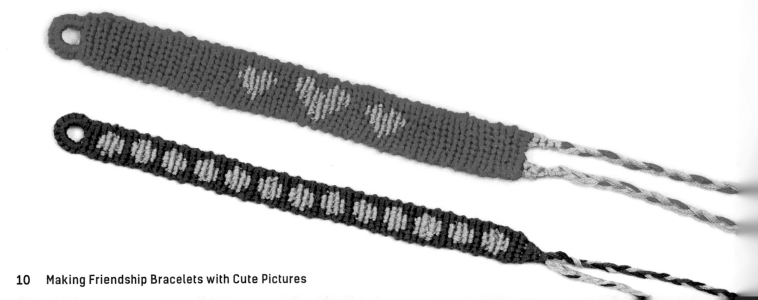

Intermediate Bracelets

For designs with a few simple color changes, you can choose to knot your picture all in the same color, and then go back and stitch over or duplicate-stitch small details on top of the finished bracelet stitches (see page 19). If you prefer to knot all the detail into your design, use floater strands, which are strands you work into the top loop.

This technique works best when you choose a design in which only two colors switch back and forth on the same columns. The salamander design has 12 columns total—1 border on each side and 10 picture rows (**fig. 1**). Yellow and green are used interchangeably in columns 2, 3, 4, 8, 10, and 11. If you are knotting over a doubled thread pair of yellow and green, knot with the green for the salamander and let the yellow float. Then knot with the yellow for the detailing and let the green float.

1 Cut 1 strand from the background/border color. Cut 5 strands from green, which will give you ten salamander strands. Cut 3 strands from yellow for the small details (**fig. 2a**). When you arrange the strands to make the top loop, place a yellow strand next to green strands 1, 2, and 4 (on the chart, these are columns 2, 3, and 5) (**fig. 2b**).

2 Make the top loop and fold the bracelet in half. Instead of 2 border and 10 green picture strands, you now have 16 picture strands (10 green, 6 yellow) (**fig. 3a**). However, you're still only going to be knotting over the 12 total rows (2 border and 10 picture strands). How is that? Instead of knotting over a single strand on rows, 2, 3, 5, 8, 10, and 11, you will knot the working strand over the green and yellow strands together (**fig. 3b**).

3 When you get to the yellow knot in the chart, simply use the yellow strand to knot over the border/background color (**fig. 4**). For the next row, switch back the green strand to finish the salamander body knots for the remainder of that row. Once you've completed the detail color for that entire row—in this case yellow—continue knotting over the doubled floss for several rows where it falls in a background knot. You can either clip it out or keep it doubled all the way to the end of the bracelet and use it to create wider braid ties.

> ### Tip
> Floss is relatively forgiving, and knotting over a doubled strand does not affect the design from the front. It only creates a very slight channel on the back side of the bracelet.

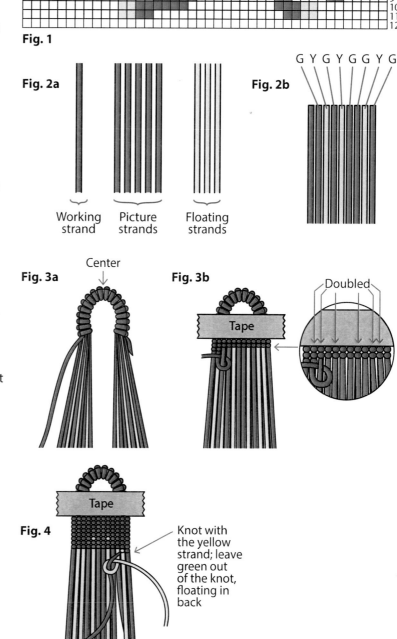

Fig. 1

Fig. 2a

Working strand Picture strands Floating strands

Fig. 2b

G Y G Y G G Y G

Fig. 3a

Center

Fig. 3b

Tape

Doubled

Fig. 4

Tape

Knot with the yellow strand; leave green out of the knot, floating in back

Advanced Bracelets

Advanced picture bracelets have several different floss colors often in one column of the designs. While there are different ways to accomplish this technique, the best option is to secure a new color to the existing strand to the wrong side of the bracelet with tape. Follow these instructions to learn the technique in full detail.

1 Isolate the existing strand (**fig. 1a**). Fold it to the wrong side of the bracelet and secure it with a small piece of tape (**fig. 1b**).

2 Make sure the new strand of floss is long enough to complete all the areas of the bracelet that you need to knot in that color. Leave a tail approximately 3" (7.62cm) long and tape it on the wrong side of your bracelet, aligning it in the slot of the old strand (**fig. 2**). There is no need to tie it off at this point.

3 Continue knotting the bracelet with the new color as the chart dictates. Depending on the design, you may need to pull the new color strand to the wrong side of the bracelet to secure it out of the way; then bring the original strand back into place, switching back and forth as the chart dictates.

4 As you work through the chart, add colors as needed, following steps 1 through 3.

5 In most cases, once you come to the end of the picture section on the bracelet, you will be finishing the bracelet with several rows using the working strand, as you did to start the bracelet. At this point, you can leave any new color strands in place and knot over those to finish the bracelet and tails, making sure they are long enough (**fig. 3**). The color doesn't really matter, as the working strand will cover it.

6 Carefully remove any tape from the back of the bracelet where you may have introduced new strands, knot together the loose ends, and dot with an anti-fraying solution. For added security, weave the tail ends through the back before cutting off the excess floss. (Refer to Weaving Strand Ends on page 17.)

If your final color strands are not long enough, fold them to the underside of your work and secure, pull your original picture base strands back into position and finish knotting the bracelet. Just make sure you are knotting over the same number of strands you started with.

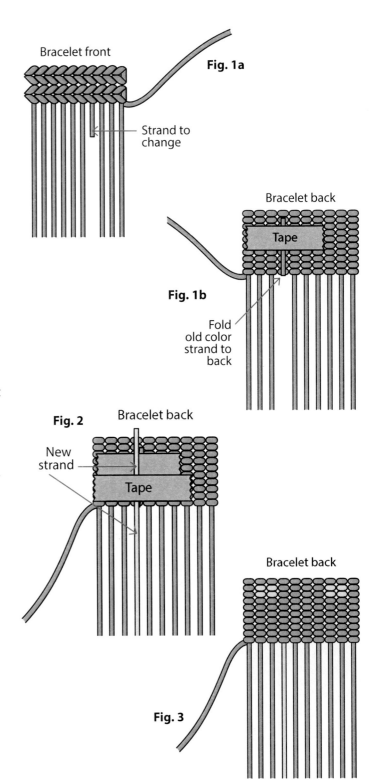

Bracelet front

Fig. 1a

Strand to change

Bracelet back

Tape

Fig. 1b

Fold old color strand to back

Fig. 2

Bracelet back

New strand

Tape

Bracelet back

Fig. 3

Multicolor Bracelets

To avoid extra color changes that aren't necessarily needed, take a look at your graph before you begin and determine what colors are introduced first. I will be using an owl design as an example for this technique.

1 In the owl chart, you will work over 12 strands, so cut 6 strands 48" (122cm) long (**fig. 1a**). Cut 1 border/background strand from the blue knotting skein (introduced on column 1), 1 strand from tan (introduced on rows 2 and 11), 4 strands from brown (introduced on row 8) (**fig. 1b**). This lets you to knot the entire wing before having to work in more tan strands for the owl.

2 Since this design is identical from the midpoint on each side, simply fold the brown/gray strands under after completing the first wing, taping or pinning them out of the way (**fig. 2a**). Once you've added in the tan strands (**fig. 2b**) and the body of the owl is complete, fold the tan strands to the back and bring the brown strands to the front.

3 There are two ways to add the beak and eye detail. The first is to introduce the yellow and orange strands in the same manner as the tan, folding tan strands back and forth as needed. The second is to knot the owl body entirely in tan, and once complete, go back and duplicate-stitch the eye and beak detail (see page 19).

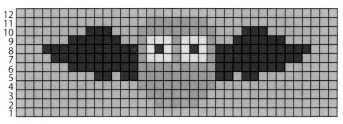

Fig. 1a

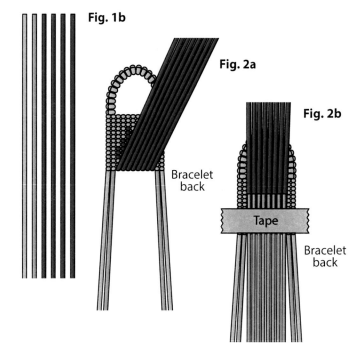

Fig. 1b

Fig. 2a

Fig. 2b

Bracelet back

Tape

Bracelet back

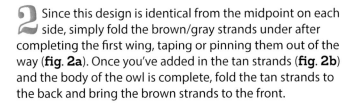

Fig. A

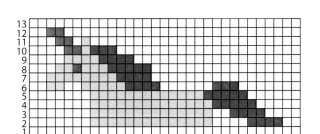

Fig. B

The orange strand is in the wrong slot

Adding Color Alternative

It's not always particularly helpful to cut the first color introduced, especially if it's only a small part of the design, such as the orange horn in the unicorn illustration.

The orange horn is introduced first on the 12th strand (**fig. A**). Let's say you cut a long strand of orange at the beginning with the others colors. Once you've created your loop and have folded the strands in half, you would end up with an orange strand in the second spot rather than the pink strand needed there. Eventually, you would have to swap out to pink (**fig. B**).

It's better, in this case, to cut pink strands for the bracelet base and do one of three things. First, you could introduce the colors as needed, taping them in and tying off when finished. Second, cut double strands for the horn and knot as one, as instructed in the intermediate technique (see page 11). Third, duplicate-stitch the horn and eye details.

Ending a Bracelet

Friendship bracelets can be finished in three different ways. The style you choose will depend on your bracelet's size and your personal preference.

Option 1

This simple option works well with any bracelet width.

1 Divide the strands at the end of bracelet into two groups. One side will have the knotting strand and the next three strands. The second group will have the remaining four strands. Braid the left group of strands together, treating one set of 2 strands as one strand (**fig. 1**). Repeat on the right group.

2 Secure each braid with an OK. Trim any excess strands (**fig. 2**).

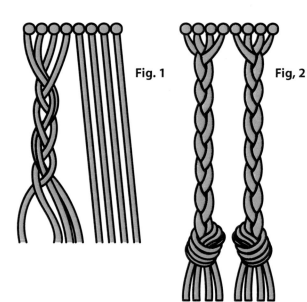

Fig. 1   Fig, 2

Saving Scraps

You'll have a lot of floss clippings left from tails or strands cut from bracelets that have an odd number of rows. Don't throw them away! Instead, keep them and organize by color in small zipper-top bags. This way, when you need to add a color on a different bracelet, you'll likely have a piece already cut that's just the right size.

Option 2

This works well with bracelets that have 9 or more strands.

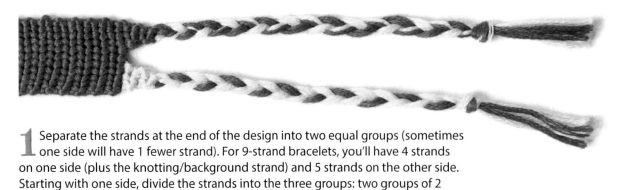

1 Separate the strands at the end of the design into two equal groups (sometimes one side will have 1 fewer strand). For 9-strand bracelets, you'll have 4 strands on one side (plus the knotting/background strand) and 5 strands on the other side. Starting with one side, divide the strands into the three groups: two groups of 2 strands and the outermost single strand.

2 Using the outermost strand, work two OK over the first 2 strands (**fig. 1**), then the second 2 strands, then work back the opposite direction in the same manner. OK for three rows (**fig. 2**).

3 Separate the strands again into three sections and braid for 3"–4" (7.6–10.2cm). OK the end of the braided strand and cut a fringed end (**fig. 3**). Repeat all steps for the opposite side.

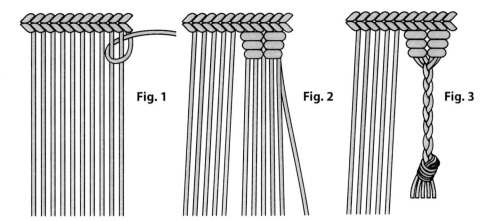

Fig. 1 Fig. 2 Fig. 3

Option 3

Tapering the ends of a bracelet into a triangular shape is a pretty option for a wider bracelet, but you need to keep in mind that it will add length to the bracelet depending on where you begin to taper.

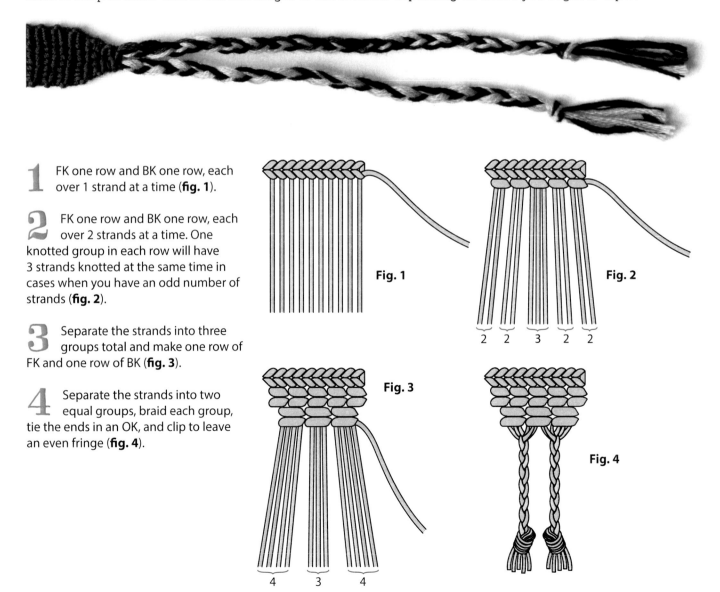

1 FK one row and BK one row, each over 1 strand at a time (**fig. 1**).

2 FK one row and BK one row, each over 2 strands at a time. One knotted group in each row will have 3 strands knotted at the same time in cases when you have an odd number of strands (**fig. 2**).

3 Separate the strands into three groups total and make one row of FK and one row of BK (**fig. 3**).

4 Separate the strands into two equal groups, braid each group, tie the ends in an OK, and clip to leave an even fringe (**fig. 4**).

Fig. 1

Fig. 2

2 2 3 2 2

Fig. 3

Fig. 4

4 3 4

Troubleshooting

These helpful tips and solutions to common occurrences and frequently asked questions will help you on your crafting journey to make the most beautiful bracelets.

Reading Charted Designs

Each square on a chart is equal to one FK or one BK. It's easy to accidentally skip a row and throw off your design, especially when making your first picture bracelets. To stay on track, photocopy and print out your graph, and use a pencil to mark through each row on your chart as you finish it. If you're working directly from the book pages, use a sticky note and move it along the chart row by row as you finish.

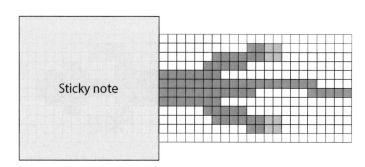

Replacing/Adding a Strand

If you run out of a color while knotting or a strand frays and breaks, you will need to add a new length. Tying a new strand to the existing one will sometimes cause the strands to pull to the right side of your work and leave an unsightly lump. Instead, try this tape method that works much better.

1 Isolate your short strand (**fig. 1**). Fold the strand to the underside of the bracelet; leave a tail at least 3" (7.6cm) long if possible (or as long as remains on the strand). Secure with a small piece of tape (**fig. 2**).

2 Grab a new strand of matching floss, making sure it's long enough to complete your bracelet, plus an extra 3" (7.6cm) for a tail. Tape this new strand directly over the taped old floss end on the underside of your bracelet (so you're essentially layering the tape and aligning the new strand in the slot of the old strand) (**fig. 3**). There is no need to tie off the two tails yet.

3 Continue knotting the bracelet with the new strand. Once you've completed your bracelet, you can carefully remove the tape, knot the ends, and dot with an anti-fraying solution. For added security, weave the tail ends through the back before cutting off the excess.

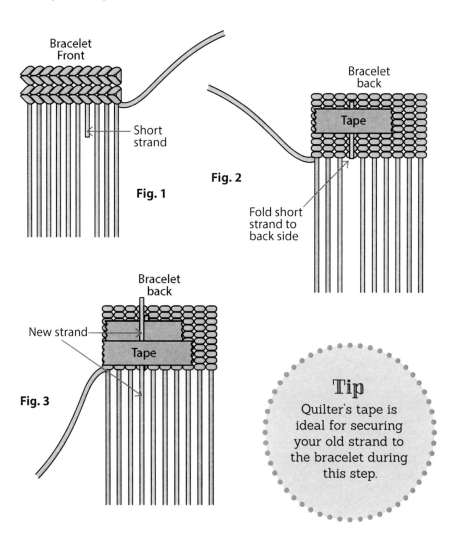

Tip
Quilter's tape is ideal for securing your old strand to the bracelet during this step.

Weaving Strand Ends

If you've added a strand of floss to the bracelet, you're going to have a tail to deal with.

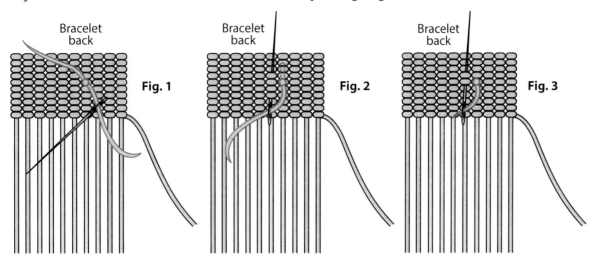

1 Once you've tied the ends of the replacement strand to the old strand, dot the knot with an anti-fraying solution to keep it from loosening. Thread the tail ends through a needle (**fig. 1**). Weave through the back of the bracelet and clip off the excess strand (**fig. 2**).

2 If your ends are so short that they don't have slack to maneuver, first weave the needle into the back of the bracelet, then thread the strand through the eye (**fig. 3**). Pull the needle through the weave and clip off the strand end.

Stitch Tension for Colors

It is possible for colors to accidentally switch as you are knotting, usually caused by pulling one strand tighter than the other. To fix this problem, do one of the following:

• Pull the *accent* strand tighter to allow the background strand color to show.

• Pull the *background* strand tighter to allow the accent strand color to show.

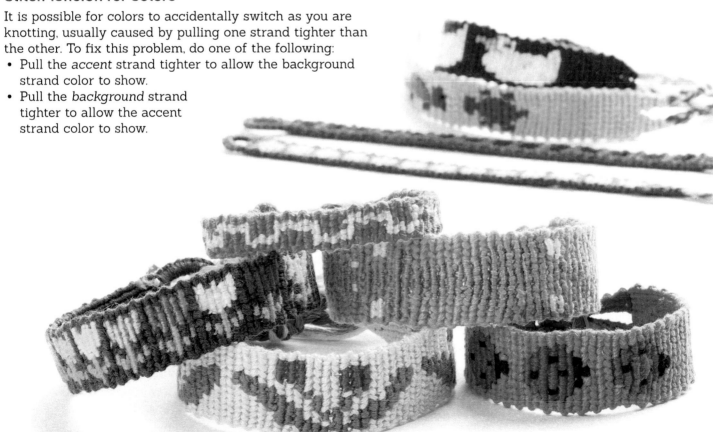

How to Fluff a Stitch

Sometimes—especially for beginners—you may notice that your knots will differ in size. Use a safety pin or sewing needle to gently pull any smaller knots to the top.

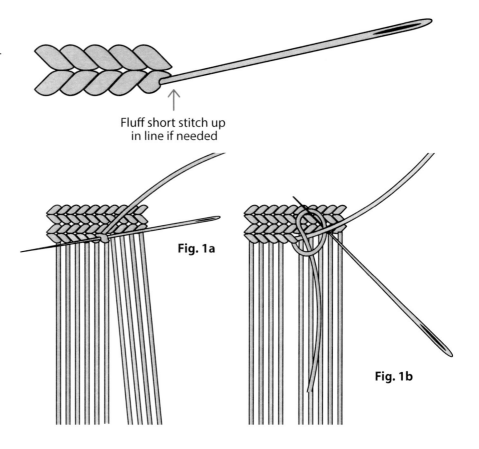

Fluff short stitch up
in line if needed

Removing Stitches

If you notice a mistake in your knotting, you can easily "unknot" your bracelet, one knot at a time, but it takes time and patience. Any pin or sewing needle is helpful for loosening knots. A darner with a blunt tip will help avoid damage to the strands, but a sharper point is sometimes needed to loosen a tight knot.

Place the tip of a pin or needle underneath the knot and work to gently coax the knot loose with the point of the needle, keeping the floss strands together (**fig. 1a**). Once the knot begins to loosen, use the needle to enlarge the loop (**fig. 1b**). Pull out the knot and rework.

Fig. 1a

Fig. 1b

Tangled Strands

Starting with strands secured on a clothespin or bobbin can help prevent knotted and twisted strands, but it does still happen.

To remove a knot, first gently and calmly work with your fingers to pull the twists loose. When you look closely you can usually begin to see which strand has a problem. Then use a safety pin or sewing needle to help loosen the strands. Finally, loosen the knots. Remember . . . be gentle and calm.

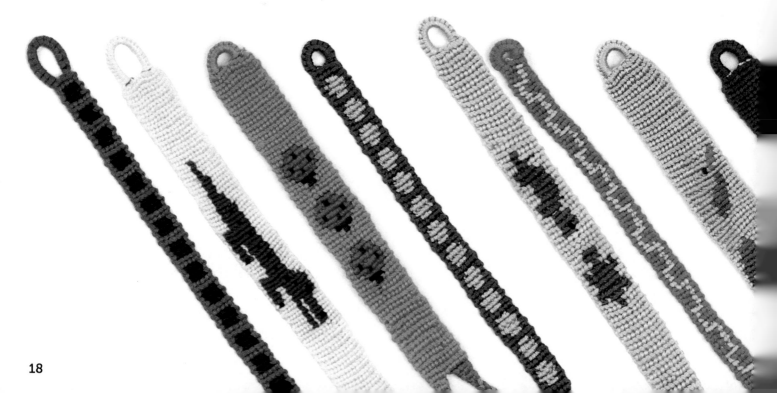

Covering a Stitch (or Duplicate Stitch)

If you realize you've made a mistake four or five rows ago, here's a quick way to cover the incorrect stitches.

1 Thread a needle with the correct floss color. Weave it through the back of your bracelet near the area to be fixed (**fig. 1a**) and come up next to the incorrect knot (**fig. 1b**).

2 Take a stitch over the top of the wrong color stitch, guiding the needle back through to the wrong side (**fig. 2a**). If you have more than one wrong-color stitch in a row, come back up on the far side of the second incorrect stitch and guide the needle back on the opposite side to cover that stitch. You are essentially working a backstitch to cover the wrong-colored stitches with the correct floss color. Continue backstitching over as many stitches as needed, fluffing with the tip of your needle as needed (**fig. 2b**).

3 Once all your stitches are covered, guide the needle to the backside of the bracelet, weave the strand back to your starting point, tie off in a small knot, secure the knot with a dot of anti-fraying solution, and clip the tails (**fig. 3**).

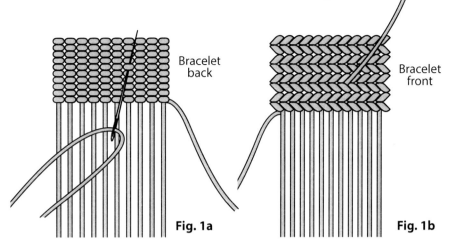

Bracelet back

Bracelet front

Fig. 1a　　**Fig. 1b**

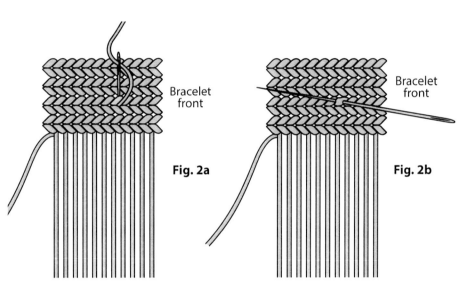

Bracelet front

Bracelet front

Fig. 2a　　**Fig. 2b**

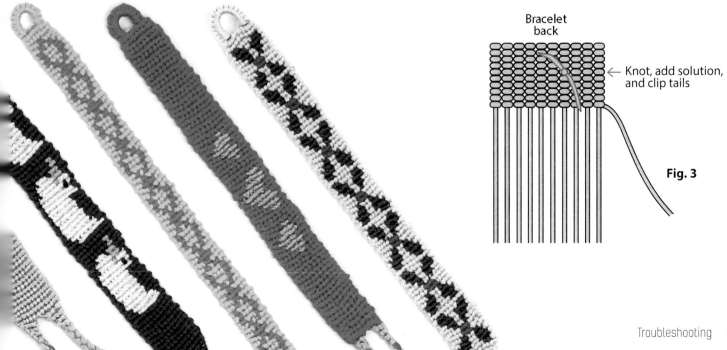

Bracelet back

← Knot, add solution, and clip tails

Fig. 3

Picture Bracelet Charts

This section contains a bunch of designs for you to use to create your bracelets. The first section contains simple geometric designs that you can use to create fun bracelets that make great filler bracelets to wear with others. The other sections share more complicated designs.

Geometric Designs

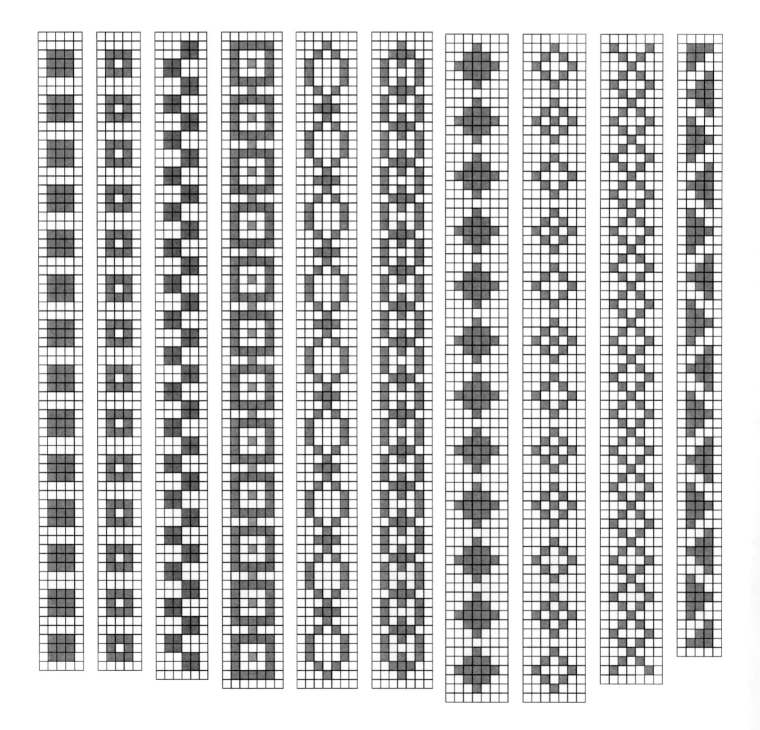

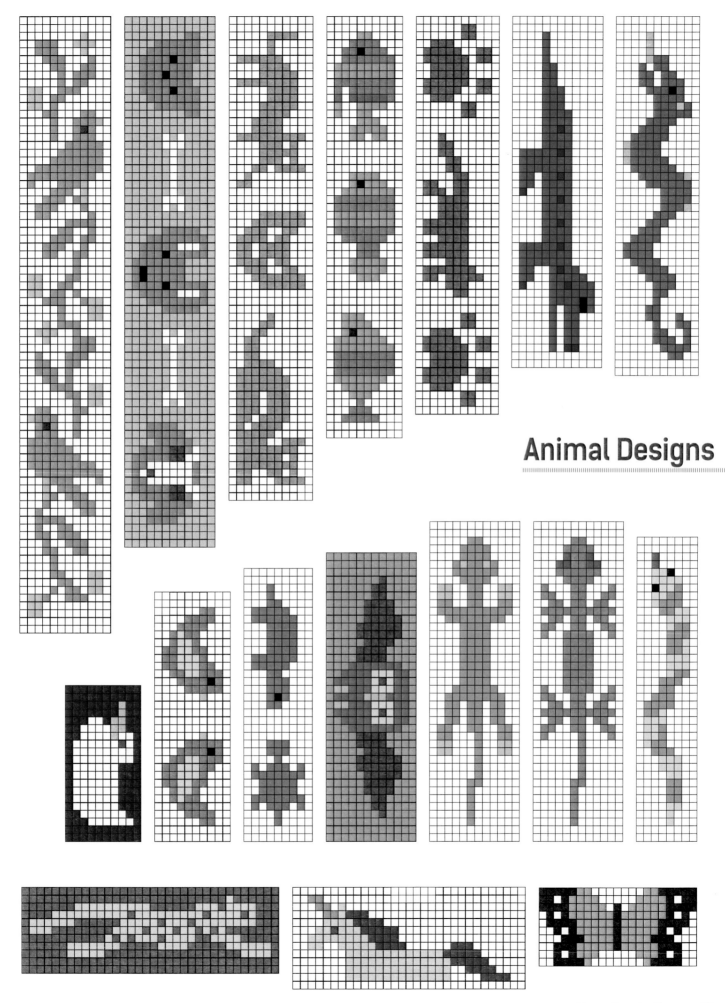

Animal Designs

Seasonal Designs

Valentine's Day

Mother's Day / Father's Day

St. Patrick's Day

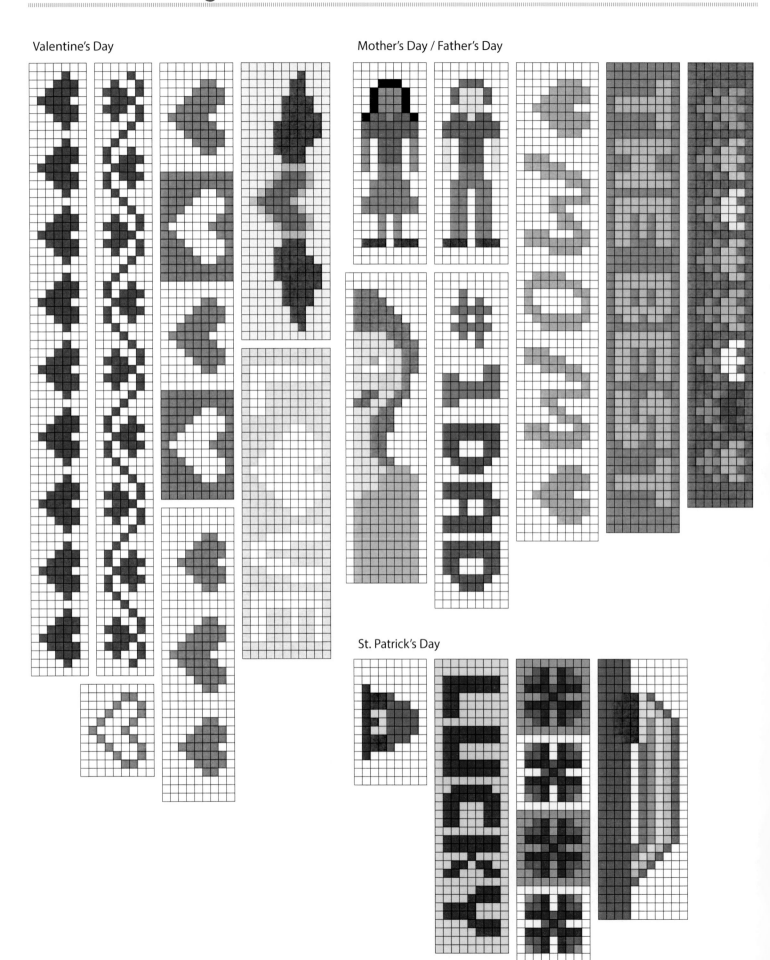

Easter / Springtime

4th of July / Summertime

Awareness Month

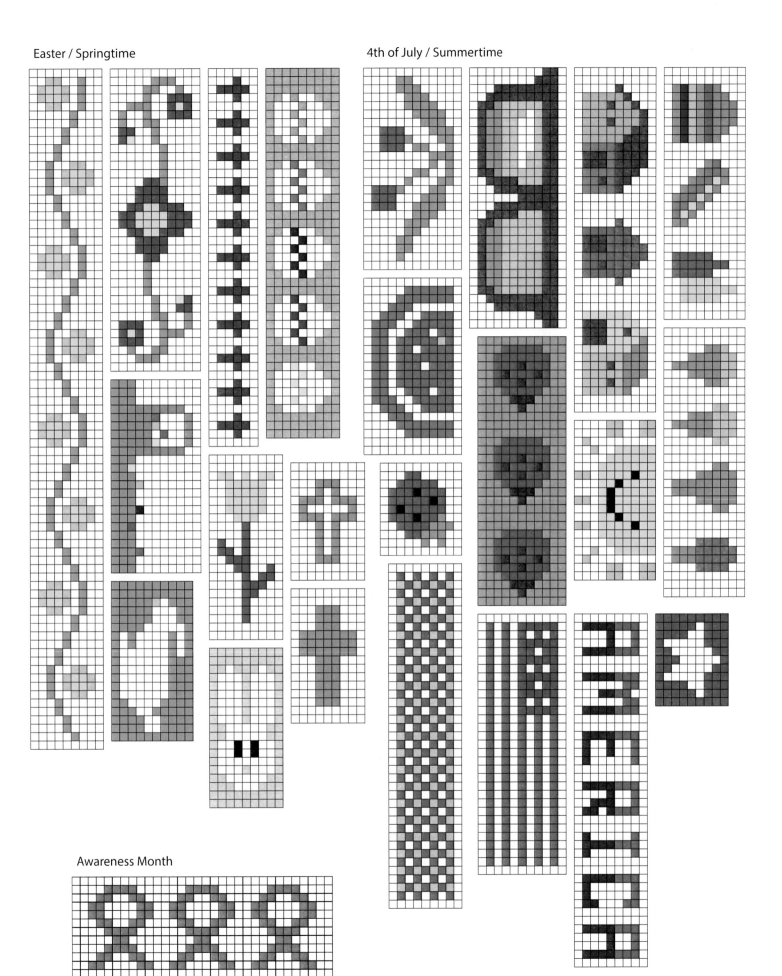

Halloween

Christmas

Hanukkah

Kwanzaa

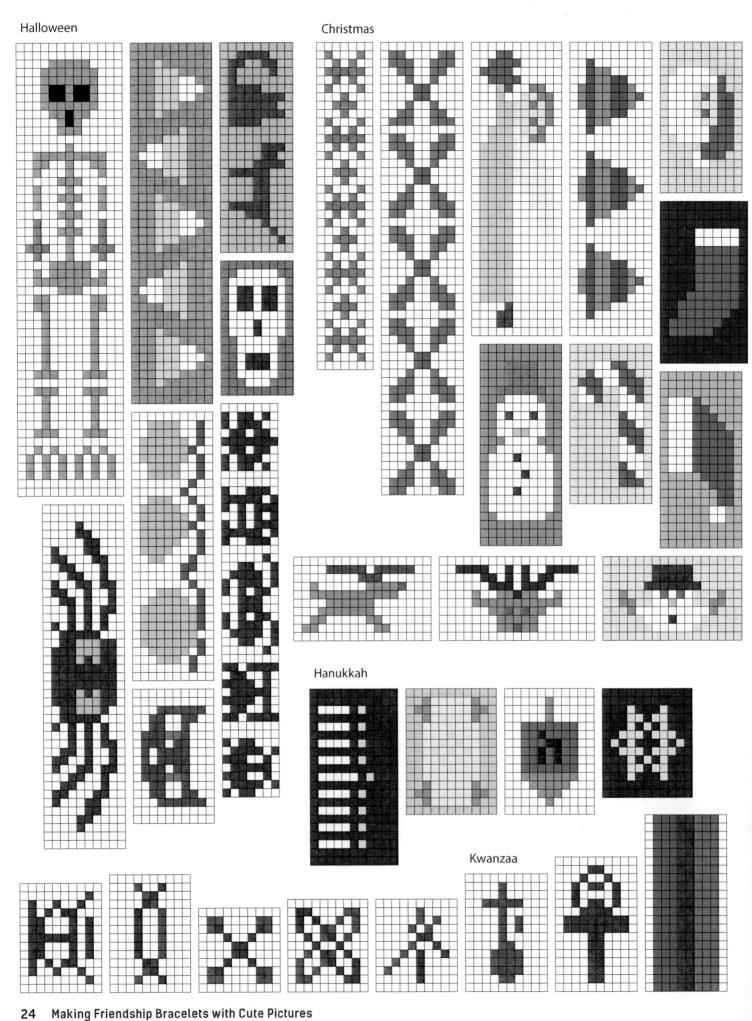

Making Friendship Bracelets with Cute Pictures